"WANTED DEAD or ALIVE"

The True Story of Harriet Tubman

Original title: Runaway Slave

by Ann McGovern

Pictures by R. M. POWERS
Cover art by BRIAN PINKNEY

SCHOLASTIC INC.

New York   Toronto   London   Auckland   Sydney

Remembering —
Cynthia Wesley
Denise McNair
Carol Robertson
Addie Mae Collins

ISBN 0-590-44212-0

12 11 10 9 8 7 6 5 4   3 4 5 6/9

Printed in the U.S.A.   08

Can a human being be owned by another person — the way a cow or a horse is owned? People who used to have slaves thought so. Like a cow or a horse, a slave must work for the person who owns him, they said. Like a cow or a horse, a slave could be sold by his owner.

We do not have slaves in this country now. No one has a right to treat another human being like a cow or a horse.

But once there was slavery in this country. Thousands of Black people were kidnaped in Africa. Ships carried them to America to be sold as slaves. The children and grand-children of these Blacks were kept as slaves.

Almost all the slaves worked in the South on big farms called *plantations*.

In the North, most farms were small, and the farmers did not need slaves. Most Northern states made laws against owning slaves. The Blacks there were free.

Even in the South there were free Blacks. Some slaves in the South were freed by their masters. Some slaves ran away to be free.

This is the story of one slave who ran away. But running away was not all she did. This story tells how Harriet Tubman helped other slaves become free.

Who Was Harriet Tubman?

More than a hundred years ago, in the year 1820, a baby girl was born. She was born in a small cabin. The cabin was on a plantation in the state of Maryland.

The baby's mother was Old Rit. The baby's father was Ben. They were Negro slaves.

All the slaves on this Maryland plantation belonged to the master, Edward Brodas. The master owned many slaves. And now he owned this baby.

Her real name was Araminta. The people on the plantation called her Minty when she was a little girl. They called her Harriet when she was older.

Later she was called by another name. All over the land she was known as Moses. People said she was like Moses of the Bible. When his people were slaves in Egypt, Moses led them out of Egypt. He led them to freedom. And Harriet Tubman — like Moses — led hundreds of slaves to freedom.

At Miss Susan's

Harriet could not fall asleep. Underneath the blanket, the dirt floor was hard, but she was used to that.

Her brothers were talking, but she was used to that too.

It was their words that were keeping her awake. Terrible, scary words.

"They say the master has no more money," one of her brothers said.

"That's why so many of our people are gone," another brother said. "He sells the slaves to get money. Or he sends them away to work for other plantation owners."

"Who will be next? One of us?"

"Shush. You'll scare the little ones."

Harriet whispered in the dark. "Please, Lord," she prayed. "Don't let the master send my brothers and sisters away. Please, Lord."

The next day the air was warm. The sun was golden. It was too nice a day to worry.

But Harriet thought of the words she heard in the dark. *Who will be next? One of us?*

That same morning a woman came to the plantation to see the master.

"I want a girl to take care of my baby," Miss Susan told Edward Brodas. "I can only pay you a few pennies a week for her."

"I have just the girl for you," Mr. Brodas said. "She's only seven, but she can do the job."

Miss Susan's wagon took Harriet farther and farther away from the plantation. What would her family say, she wondered. How would they feel when they learned she had been sent away?

There had been no time to say good-bye.

Harriet found out right away what work she

had to do. Miss Susan told her to dust and sweep.

Harriet knew how to sweep. She had often swept the dirt floor in her own cabin.

But she did not know how to dust. She had never learned, for there was no fine furniture in a slave's cabin. Miss Susan whipped her for not knowing the right way to dust.

Every day Harriet cleaned the house and ran errands. Every night Harriet rocked the baby. Harriet had to make sure that the baby did not wake up and cry.

The baby slept in a cradle near Miss Susan's

bed. Above the bed was a shelf where Miss Susan kept her whip made of rawhide. If the baby woke up and began to cry, Miss Susan reached for the whip. Harriet was whipped so often she had scars on her neck for the rest of her life.

One day she ran away. But she did not know how to get home. Years later Harriet told what happened.

"One morning Miss Susan had the baby, and I stood by the table waiting until I was to take it. Near me was a bowl full of sugar lumps. I never had anything good. And that sugar,

right by me, did look so nice, and my mistress'
back was turned to me. So I just put my fingers
in the bowl to take one lump, and she turned
and saw me. The next minute she had the rawhide down.

"I gave one jump out the door. I ran and
I ran. By and by I came to a great pigpen.
There was an old sow there, and eight or ten
little pigs. I tumbled over the high part of the
fence and fell on the ground.

"And there I stayed from Friday until the
next Tuesday, fighting with those little pigs for
the potato peelings. By Tuesday I was so

starved I knew I had to go back to my mistress. I didn't have anywhere else to go, even though I knew what was coming."

By now Harriet was very weak and was not able to do much work. So Miss Susan brought her back to Edward Brodas.

"She wasn't worth six pennies," Miss Susan told him.

Follow the North Star

Harriet was growing up. By the time she was eleven years old, she was very strong. She worked from sunrise to sunset. She plowed the cornfields. She loaded heavy wood into wagons. She worked as hard as a man, but she was happier than she had ever been. For she loved being out of doors.

Out of doors she felt almost free.

Free. Harriet thought of freedom all the time. Many slaves had tried to run away. The ones that were caught were brought back. They were beaten. Then they were put in chains and sent to plantation owners who lived in states even farther South — where it would be harder to escape. There they were put to work on the big cotton or rice plantations.

At night many slaves came to Old Rit's cabin. They talked in whispers. They sang softly of the states up North — and beyond. Of a land called Canada. Men could be free up North, they said.

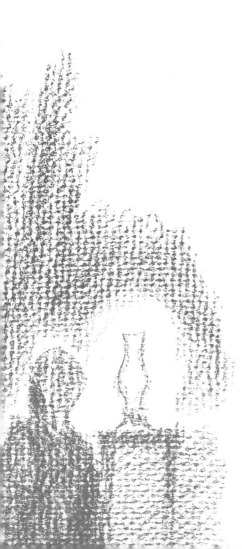

"How do you get there?" Harriet asked.

"By Underground Railroad," they told her.

"Is there really a train that runs underneath the earth?" she asked.

"No," one of the slaves said. "We call it *underground* because it is secret. There are special secret roads and paths that lead North. There are people who hide runaway slaves and help them on their way. These people hate slavery. They are called *station masters*. Their houses are called *stations*."

Harriet listened. Her eyes had a faraway look.

The man said, "The Underground Railroad has *conductors*, too. The conductors are people who come secretly to the South. They lead groups of slaves to freedom. They lead them North — always North. Always following the North Star."

From the door of her cabin, Harriet could see the bright star, shining like a far-off beam of hope in the night sky.

Follow the North Star to freedom.

Some day she would.

Trouble!

One evening when Harriet was thirteen, she was working in a cornfield.

Nearby stood the overseer. It was his job to see that the slaves did their work well. If they didn't, he used the long whip he always carried.

While she worked, Harriet kept looking at one of the slaves. Something was wrong. He wasn't doing much work.

Suddenly he began to run across the cornfield. The overseer shouted at him to come back. But the slave kept running. The overseer ran after him. Harriet knew there would be trouble. She followed the two men to the village store.

The overseer wanted to whip the slave right there in the store. He saw Harriet and told her to help him hold the slave so he could tie him and whip him.

Harriet shook her head *no*. At that moment the slave ran out the door. Quickly Harriet stood in the doorway to stop the overseer from running after him.

The overseer picked up a heavy iron weight. He threw it at the slave. But the iron struck Harriet's head instead. She fell to the ground.

For months Old Rit and Ben did not know whether their daughter would live or die.

While Harriet was sick, her master tried to sell her. But nobody wanted a sick slave. Nobody wanted a slave like Harriet, who would not obey an overseer.

Day by day Harriet grew stronger. But she never completely recovered. There was a deep scar where the iron had hit her. And for the rest of her life she had strange sleeping spells. Harriet never knew when or where she would suddenly fall asleep.

John Tubman

When Harriet was well enough to work again, there was a new master. Edward Brodas had died.

The new master sent Harriet to work for John Stewart, a builder. For a few years she worked in his house. Then she worked in the fields.

John Stewart could hardly believe what he saw. Harriet was shorter than most women. But she was stronger than most men. She lifted heavy wooden barrels as if they were made of paper. She cut more wood in a day than any other slave.

Stewart showed her off. He made Harriet show her strength in front of his friends. Harriet hated that.

But she felt lucky to be working for Stewart because he let her "hire her time." That meant Harriet could work for others. She had to give Stewart fifty dollars a year. If she made more money than that, she could keep it.

Stewart and his friends were not the only ones who admired Harriet's strength. Workers in the field looked at her in wonder.

One of them was John Tubman. He was a Negro, but he was not a slave like the others. His mother and father had been freed by their master before John was born. John had never been a slave. When he worked, he was paid for the job. And he was allowed to keep all the money he made.

Harriet had never known a man like John —tall and laughing and *free.* Soon after they met, they were married.

Harriet was happy now, except for one thing.

She wanted more than ever to live in freedom. Surely John would want her to be free too.

She began to make plans for them to run away.

By day Harriet thought about escaping to the North. At night she dreamed about it. In her dreams she saw men on horseback, riding in the night. She heard mothers and children scream as they were torn from each other.

Then the dream changed. She saw a land with a line through it. On one side of the line was slavery. On the other side was freedom. She dreamed that beautiful white ladies held

out their hands across the line to welcome her to freedom.

She told the dreams to John. But he laughed at her. He said he didn't want to hear her foolish talk about running away.

Harriet did not understand. John was free. Didn't he want his wife to be free too?

At night she looked up at the sky—at the bright North Star that would guide her to freedom. And she knew that she could not share her dreams and plans with John Tubman. She had to go on without him.

"I'm Going to Leave You"

One day, about four years after she was married, Harriet learned that she was going to be sold. She was going to be sent farther South to work on a big cotton plantation.

This was the time to escape. This was the time to run away to the North. Harriet remembered the name of a white woman who had once promised to help her. The woman lived in Bucktown, not far away. Her home was a station on the Underground Railroad. Was the woman still there? Would she remember Harriet? Harriet decided not to wait another day.

Two of Harriet's brothers were going to be sold too. They said they would escape with her.

Harriet could not say good-bye to anyone — not even to her mother and father. An escape had to be secret.

That evening she walked past the slave

cabins, and in her low, deep voice she sang:

> When that old chariot comes,
> I'm going to leave you.
> I'm bound for the promised land.
> Friends, I'm going to leave you.

Later, after she was gone, her friends and family thought about that song. They knew it was Harriet's good-bye message. They knew that the promised land was the North.

The sky was clear, the North Star was bright when Harriet and her brothers started out. She was glad that her brothers were with her. There was danger ahead. But she did not feel so frightened with them along.

Harriet led the way, and they started through the woods. Her brothers jumped at every sound. They were afraid the slave-catchers would be after them — with dogs to track them down. After a little while, the brothers stopped. They whispered together. Then they told Harriet they were turning back. They said it was too dangerous and that they would surely be caught.

Harriet tried to make them change their mind. Yes, it was dangerous, she said. But wasn't freedom worth the dangers?

But they would not go on.

Now Harriet was alone, but she didn't feel alone. She felt that God would take care of her.

"I'm going to hold steady unto You," she prayed. "And You've got to see me through."

All that night she walked through the woods toward Bucktown. She was tired, frightened, and hungry. Was she being followed? Harriet listened for the pounding of horses' hoofs. But the only pounding she heard was the sound of her own frightened heartbeats.

She listened for the barking of the slave-catcher's dogs. But she heard only the sounds of the forest — the running brook, the blowing leaves.

At last Harriet came to Bucktown. She found the house of the woman who had promised to help her. The woman remembered Harriet. She invited Harriet in and gave her some food. She told Harriet where to go next. She told her how to find the next station on the Underground Railroad.

Harriet was traveling the Underground Railroad at last. Traveling North to freedom.

By day she hid. She slept wherever she could. One day she hid in an attic. Another day she hid in a pile of potatoes under a cabin floor.

By night she moved North. One night she

traveled in the bottom of a farmer's wagon. She hid under a pile of corn. One night she crossed a river in a rowboat. It was so dark she could not see the man who rowed the boat.

Many nights she walked alone through the woods and the swamps. On clear nights the North Star was her guide. And when clouds hid the stars, she found her way North by touching the trees. She knew that thick moss grew on the northern side of the trees.

After days and nights of walking and hiding, she reached the state of Pennsylvania. Now she was safe. Nobody would make her go back to

Maryland. Pennsylvania was a free state. No one in that state was allowed to own slaves. And most people in Pennsylvania were glad to help runaway slaves.

"I looked at my hands to see if I was the same person, now I was free," she said later. "There was such a glory over everything. The sun came like gold through the trees and over the fields, and I felt like I was in Heaven."

Then she thought of her family back in Maryland. And she made a promise to herself.

"I had crossed the line of which I had so long been dreaming," she said later. "I was free, but there was no one to welcome me to the land of freedom. I was a stranger in a strange land. And my home, after all, was down with the old folks and my brothers and sisters. But I was free and *they* should be free. I would make a home in the North, and with the Lord helping me, I would bring them all there!"

Harriet Tubman, Conductor

Harriet walked on to the city of Philadelphia. She had never lived in a city before. At first Philadelphia seemed big and unfriendly. But Harriet soon made friends and found work.

For more than a year she cooked, cleaned, and scrubbed floors. She saved every penny she could.

In Philadelphia, she heard of a place where slaves who had escaped could get help. Harriet often went there after work. She met other slaves who had run away from their masters. She listened to their stories. And sometimes she heard news of her family.

In December, 1850, she heard about her sister, her sister's husband, and their two children. They too had tried to run away. They had got as far as Baltimore, Maryland. But no place in Maryland was safe for a runaway slave. Now they had to get to Philadelphia.

Harriet went secretly to Baltimore. And

from Baltimore she set out for Philadelphia, leading two grownups, a small child, and a baby.

Her own escape had been dangerous and frightening. But then she had only herself to worry about. Now she had to worry about four other people.

It was winter, and snow lay on the ground. They walked and walked until their shoes split open and their feet became numb with the cold.

There was an extra danger in traveling with small children. What if they cried? A slave-catcher might hear! Harriet was prepared

for this danger. At night she gave the two children medicine to put them to sleep.

Through the long cold nights, the grownups took turns carrying the sleeping children. By day friendly people — members of the Underground Railroad — hid them in their homes.

No one knew how frightened Harriet was. Her courage gave the others the strength to go on.

At last Harriet and her little group reached Philadelphia. She had made her first trip as conductor on the Underground Railroad.

But runaway slaves were no longer safe in

Philadelphia or in any other place in the North. A new law said runaway slaves had to be sent back to their masters in the South. Anyone helping the runaways could be made to pay a large fine or be put in jail. This law was the Fugitive Slave Law of 1850.

Some people who owned slaves said that now their slaves would not dare run away. But they were wrong.

More and more slaves escaped. More and more people helped the slaves to freedom. Now there were Underground Railroad stations all the way to Canada. And in Canada runaway slaves were safe.

The new law did not stop Harriet. She made many more trips back to the South. She helped many slaves escape from their masters.

Nighttime, Daytime

It is five years before the beginning of the Civil War.

On the plantations of Maryland when they talk about Harriet, they call her Moses. In the North, too, she is known as Moses.

In the little slave cabins they whisper her name and hope she will come soon. In the big plantation houses, the masters wonder, "Who is this person they call Moses?"

Nighttime. A song is sung outside the slave cabins:

> Go down, Moses
>
> Way down to Egypt land
>
> And tell old Pharaoh
>
> To let my people go.

A slave whispers to his wife, "She is here. Get the children ready."

The next morning an overseer counts six slaves missing. Moses again!

Daytime. A Negro woman walks down the street. A big sunbonnet covers her face. She carries two chickens and walks bent over, like an old woman.

Suddenly she sees a white man coming toward her. Quickly she lets go of the chickens. The man laughs to see the old woman chasing two chickens across the road.

As soon as he is out of sight, the woman laughs too. Her trick has worked. The man did not recognize her. The man was her old master. The woman was Moses again!

Nighttime. In Wilmington, Delaware, the house of Thomas Garrett is being watched. Everyone knows he is a friend of the slaves. Everyone knows he hides them in his house. He even gives them food and money and shoes. The people

who keep watch over his house would like to catch him helping a runaway slave. They would get a reward for returning the slave to his master.

The door of Thomas Garrett's house opens. There he is! But the woman with him can't be a slave! She walks like a great lady. And her gray-silk gown and heavy gray veil are the clothes of a lady! Mr. Garrett takes her arm and leads her to his carriage. The carriage drives away — with Moses again!

Daytime. A woman sits in a railroad station. Nearby two men are talking about a big reward.

"Forty thousand dollars for Harriet Tubman, dead or alive," one of the men says.

Then the men see the Negro woman sitting in the station. They stare at the deep scar on her forehead. Quickly the woman opens a book and pretends to read it. She hears one of the men say, "That can't be the woman we want. Harriet Tubman can't read or write!"

But it *is* Harriet Tubman. It is the one they call Moses.

"Go On – or Die!"

Eleven slaves walked through the woods. They were cold and hungry. It was a dark night — so dark they could not see one another. Yet Harriet led them as if the sun were shining.

The slaves spoke in whispers. Their words were full of fear. They could hear the barking of dogs. The slave-catcher's dogs were after them! Harriet knew of a stream nearby. The night was bitter cold. But Harriet made them all wade into the freezing water. The dogs could not smell them in the water and could not track them down. The slaves stayed in the water until they no longer heard the dogs barking.

They walked for weeks and weeks. And they were still far from Canada.

They were always hungry. Harriet found apples, berries, and corn in the woods. She found fish in the river. But there was never enough food.

Harriet tried to cheer them up. She told

them they were not far from a farmhouse where they would be welcome. Plenty of food there, she said. And a warm fire.

When dawn came, she left the others hiding in the woods and went to the farmhouse. But when she knocked on the door, a strange voice answered.

"Where is the man who used to live here?" Harriet asked fearfully.

The strange voice was mean. "He had to leave — for helping slaves!"

Harriet knew she must lead her group to safety. The man had seen her. He would tell others. They would surely begin to look for her.

Harriet told the group what had happened. There was a long silence. And then a very frightened slave said, "I'm going home. We'll never get to Canada."

Harriet could not let the slave go back. It was too dangerous. The master would force him to tell about the secret Underground Railroad — the paths they walked, the houses they hid in, and the people who helped them.

From her pocket Harriet took out the gun she always carried. She pointed it at the frightened man's head. "You go on," she said in a steady voice. "You go on — or you die!"

The group went on together. They followed Harriet. She led them to a swamp. The swamp was so cold and wet, and smelled so bad, that Harriet knew no enemy would look for them there.

But Harriet hoped and prayed that a friend would come to help them. Perhaps a member of the Underground Railroad had seen her visit the house.

The slaves hid in the tall wet grass for hours, too miserable to talk. Harriet prayed silently, "I'm going to hold steady unto You, and You've got to see me through."

At dusk they saw a man walking on a path at the edge of the swamp. He seemed to be

talking to himself, but Harriet heard his words. "My wagon stands in the barnyard across the way," he said. "The horse is in the stable. The harness hangs on a nail."

The man walked away.

A friend *had* come!

When it was dark, Harriet went to the barnyard. There was the wagon. There was the horse. And in the wagon were food and blankets for all.

She hurried to tell the others. Tears of joy streamed down their faces. "Praise God," they said.

They were on their way to freedom. And Harriet was leading them there.

A Sad Christmas for Old Rit

One day a letter came to a plantation in
Maryland. It was addressed to Jacob Jackson.
In those days the postmaster opened all mail
addressed to Negroes. This letter to Jacob said,
"Read my letter to the old folks and give my
love to them. Tell my brothers to be always
watching . . . and when the good old ship of
Zion comes along, to be ready to step on
board." The letter was signed: William Henry
Jackson.

William Jackson lived up North. He was Jacob's adopted son. But William Jackson did not have any brothers! His letter made no sense to the postmaster.

Jacob Jackson was sent for. He was asked to explain what the letter meant.

Jacob read the letter. He pretended to read very slowly. Then he said, "That letter can't be for me. I can't make head or tail of it."

Jacob hurried off. He had important news to tell. That letter was from Harriet! She had never learned to write, so she had someone write for her. But Jacob knew what the letter

meant. Harriet was coming for her three brothers! They must be ready to go at any moment. "And just in time," Jacob thought. For the day after Christmas Harriet's brothers were to be sent much farther South.

Harriet reached the plantation the day before Christmas. She hid in a little shack where the corn was kept. That night her brothers met her there. They brought with them two other men who wanted freedom too.

There were wide cracks in the boards of the little shack. Harriet could peer through the cracks and see the cabin where her mother

and father lived. She had not seen Old Rit and Ben for six years. She missed them terribly.

Harriet sent the two strange men to the cabin to wake up her father. She told the men to be sure not to let her mother know they were there. Her mother would surely try to keep her three sons on the plantation. And if her mother saw Harriet, she might cry. Their hiding place might be discovered.

A little later their father Ben came to the shack to bring them some food. He talked to Harriet and her brothers. But he would not look at them.

Ben knew that after Harriet had left with her brothers, the master would send for him. "Have you seen your children?" the master might say. Ben had never told a lie in his life. He wasn't going to start lying now. No matter how badly he wanted to see Harriet and her two brothers, he never once raised his head to look at them.

The next day was Christmas. All day long it rained. All day long they waited for nightfall, when they could escape. They could see Old Rit, their mother, come to the door of her cabin. They could see her watching the road

for her boys. Every year her sons spent Christmas with her. Every year she cooked a special Christmas dinner for them.

Now they could see Old Rit watching and waiting. They could see how sad she looked when she turned and went back inside.

Harriet longed to talk to her mother, to throw her arms around her, to kiss her. But she didn't dare.

Late that evening she left her hiding place and crept up to Old Rit's cabin. She saw her mother sitting in front of the fire. Just sitting there, with her head in her hands, missing her

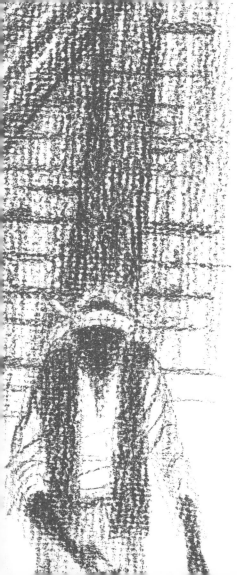

children and wondering what had happened to them.

With tears in her eyes, Harriet watched Old Rit for a long time. "Good-bye, Mother," she whispered softly — so softly her mother could not hear. "I'm coming for you soon. I'm coming to take you North." Then she turned away and went back to the others.

That night Ben came to the shack for the last time. He wanted to walk with them a little way. He had tied a handkerchief over his eyes so he would not be able to see his children.

Harriet told her father about her trips. She told him about his other children who were living free in the North. And she told him to wait for her. One day she would come for him and for Old Rit.

And she did. Old Rit and Ben were over seventy years old when they made their escape with Harriet.

Thanks to Harriet, they lived the rest of their lives in freedom.

Thanks to Harriet, more than 300 slaves reached freedom. She used to say proudly, "On my Underground Railroad I never ran my train off the track, and I never lost a passenger."

The War Years

It was 1861. The Civil War had begun. The people of the North and the people of the South fought each other. Slavery was one of the reasons they fought. It was a long and terrible war.

During the war, Harriet nursed the soldiers. The color of their skin made no difference to her. She helped any man who needed her, white or black. She found plants and roots to make

medicine. She cured many men the doctors said were too sick to be cured.

She became a spy for the Northern army. She went with the soldiers to rescue slaves from the big plantations. The story of one of her brave raids was printed on the front page of a Boston newspaper.

Two and a half years before the war was over, President Abraham Lincoln signed a document. The document was about the slaves in states that were fighting the North. It said that all the slaves in those states were forever free. This document was the Emancipation Proclamation.

The slave owners in the South did not pay attention to Lincoln's document. The South was no longer part of the United States, they said. But the slaves heard about Lincoln's words, *forever free*. Hundreds of slaves left the plantations to join the Northern army.

The war ended in April, 1865. By December of that same year, slavery was not allowed anywhere in the United States. There had been slavery in this country for almost 250 years. Now all men were free at last.

After the war, Harriet lived in the town of

Auburn, New York. She wanted only to rest and to take care of her mother and father. But the sick and the poor came to her door, and Harriet did not turn them away.

She needed money to help them. So she planted a garden and went from house to house selling vegetables. She started a home for the poor.

People came to see her from all over the land. Letters came from everywhere. She was invited to many places. The Queen of England invited her to England. But Harriet's travels were over.

Harriet Tubman lived to be more than

ninety years old. She died in Auburn, New York, in 1913.

People who pass the courthouse in Auburn can read about her on the tablet of bronze that was put up in her honor.

In cities and towns all over the land, people did not forget Harriet Tubman. They did not forget the woman who risked her life so that others might live in freedom.